MONEY

Nakayama, Kunitaka

MONEY

CONTENTS

Preface

My foremost questions concerning economy were originally "how money was invented and created out in the mankind history" and "what are the true natures of inflation and deflation". And I thought to myself we all need to start thinking from these queries, otherwise we won't find right answers to the management of economy or even solve any problems concerning national economy and finance.

So, I started to create a village of one hundred people in my imagination, hinted by an imaginary nation building by Socrates in Plato's masterpiece "Republic", in order to delve over the questions above. It is much easier to imagine a village of one hundred than to search the root cause of any problems in a huge village of over 7 billion people. And the truth to be found in such a small village can be applied to a bigger nation or even to the globe as a whole, as the same law can be applied basically as far as we are all human beings who compose a village, a nation or the entire globe.

The true nature of economy which I have thus found through building an imaginary village of one hundred is totally different from that of the conventional economy and economics. However, I am confident that the true figure which I have expounded in this short book will be exposed along with spread and development of internet technology. Why internet? You will find the answer in this book.

Let us build a true economy together both in our mind and in the real world.

PART I. Love & Intellect

1) Money

It had been my wonder and quite a big astonishment that almost none of the theories of economics has ever defined "what money is".

There has been many a thousand of theories about how to manage economy of a nation, how to get out of recession, how to control currency rate, macro-economics, micro-economics and the policies derived from them, etc., etc.

All these arguments, theories and policies are different to one another and might have some truths in them.

However, I should like to point out one ultimate pitfall or defect common to all of the theories of economics since the time of Adam Smith, father of economics, or even since the time of Plato who created an imaginary nation in his dialogue "Republic".

That defect is the lack of understanding of "what money is" or "when and under what condition money can be printed".

And if you never know true nature of money, how can you define what economy is or how economy should be managed?

But to my amazement and wonder, it seems that this has been the very tendency of all the economists so far or nobody cares what money actually is.

So, being a half philosopher by inclination, I have always tried to find out "what money is" in my philosophical quest and here is the answer which I have found by myself.

To begin with, let us imagine a very small village, such a simple one as we can imagine that could appear in the beginning of the human history to find out how money was invented and introduced in the history of mankind.

The population of the village is, let's say, one hundred people.

The dwellers of the village are living in a happy state every day without any problem.

Do we suppose that this small village needs money?

No.

The villagers are enjoying their lives doing their works and can do without money, and economy is run by barter trade. (Whether barter trade has been firmly established and prevailed all over the world before money was introduced is another question.)

So, let us increase the population and see what happens next in the village.

Up to one hundred and twenty.

Still no need for money, I should say.

What about 200? 400?

By the way I started an agriculture project in a rural village of Nepal with a native Nepali partner there in a District three-hour drive away from Kathmandu since 2010 and the population of the villages is about four hundred. They do use money everyday but it appears that they don't depend on money as much as we (developed countries) do.

So, I can fairly assert that in a village of less than five hundred people human can still manage everyday life without money. And perhaps there comes in the necessity of money when the population of a village surpasses more than five, six or seven hundred people, or maybe one thousand. But this figure is not so much of importance in this philosophical quest.

What happens when the population surpasses a certain limit is that they have to evaluate the value of each goods which every villager produces for the purpose of sale and start pricing the goods to sell in the market which would, we can imagine, naturally appear in such a situation in order to exchange goods.

This is not required when the population is one hundred, for every one of the village is quite well acquainted with everybody else and they know what neighbours produce. Moreover, the economy is run based on barter trade.

But when the population has increased up to a certain size in which each villager can't grasp what others do in the far side of the village, therefore such a situation caused the necessity of money to get out of the primitive production stage (in which every commodity reminds of its producer) to upgrade to a higher and larger level of economy (in which nobody knows who the producer of each goods is).

And in our quest the population figure is not much of importance, whether it is one hundred twenty or seven hundred.

What we have to pay our attention to most is that the necessity for money comes into being as the population increases and presumably barter trade ends in accordance with the increase of the population (or the beginning of mass production) because nobody of the village can grasp instantly who produces what.

And here is the first important point.

"Money comes into being when population increases."

And what if the population never changes or even decreases from one hundred?

We can also assume that the necessity for money never comes into being, had the village continued to exist in the state of barter trade without seeing its population increase.

Then, here comes the next important question, what is the cause of increase of population? An answer that can be universally agreed upon would be that "love" causes increase of population. And increase of population causes the necessity for money and we can imagine without any difficulty that actually it did happen in the course of history to get out of the primitive state of barter trade or primitive state of economy.

Then, can we not assert that money was invented or generated out of population increase caused by love to a large extent?

Or in short love caused the necessity for money.

And love in itself is something that has an intrinsic nature to grow, expand and increase everlastingly throughout the history of mankind towards future.

So, wherever there is love, sooner or later money must come into being at some point in the course of human history.

Therefore, love is a quintessence required for the invention of money.

Money, of course, is not love in itself, but apparently starts to appear and circulate in the village when love grows in the village and that causes the end of barter trade economy, and therefore it is quite similar to "materialisation of love" to a certain degree in this earthly world, that was invented to solve the necessity of developing the commercial system and for the mankind to climb up the ladder of inevitable course of being civilized (civilisation is to live among many) which we have witnessed by ourselves in the entire history for over some thousands of years.

Therefore we can justly conclude that this is one intrinsic nature of money.

When the village starts to get out of the barter trade, the village has gone up to a higher level of economy where it has to start mass production of any goods by which the villagers have to fulfill their increasing demands of every day life.

In order to start mass production they have to inevitably introduce division of labour which fosters specialisation of jobs and accumulation of knowledge of each labour and thus making each job more and more professional, divided and precise throughout the process.

This is the very process in which knowledge increases in every day work and profession along with growth of love in the village.

Therefore, it is quite natural that love and knowledge (and intellect) increase simultaneously.

In short love never grows alone without knowledge.

Without intellect and knowledge we can't live happily as human being.

Therefore, intellect increases simultaneously when love of the village grows up to a point where the village starts mass production and taking the course of development of commerce, thus it is also a matter of course that money was invented out by human intellect that increases along with growth of love.

Moreover, money itself is a fruit of human intellect.

So, again we can conclude that **money was invented by intellect when love grows and this is another intrinsic nature of money which can be described as;**

"Money is materialisation of human intellect and knowledge".

Therefore, in other words, money comes into being when love and intellect grow simultaneously.
And the more love and intellect grow, the more the population increases and the more acutely the demand for money is felt.

Therefore, **money is crystalisation of love and intellect.**

Now we can assert that we have found out the moment of invention of money and the very nature of money as well.
Without understanding such an aspect of the nature of money, we can't grasp how to manage economy of a nation, how to get out of recession, etc. These themes are too oftentimes argued without understanding the very nature of money.

2) Central Government and Central Bank

What we have to consider next is how the money was distributed in the beginning of the history. So, let us go back to the village of one hundred people when the money was first invented in the examination above.

In a small village like the one we are studying we can assume that there is not so much discrimination or social class as we see in our modern world today.
When money was first invented and introduced to foster the trade among the villagers, we can judge that money was simply utilised as a tool for circulating the goods produced in the village. And in the village where there is no discrimination, we can easily guess how money was distributed among the villagers.
Perhaps a leader of the village who might be the oldest declared like this;
"We have just invented a very useful tool for the sake of trade of the goods! That will be called "money" from now on. And I will allocate money equally among all the villagers. Let us use it wisely."
This might be the first and most probable declaration about the use and

allocation of money in the village we are now developing.

And this is how the money was first distributed amongst the villagers.

I will repeat;

Money was distributed among the villagers, and allocated and given to each one of the villagers hand to hand by the old leader of the village because they needed money for daily use, when love and intellect started to grow and increase in the village.

And this is how money was given to each one of our ancestors.

I will repeat. **Money was "given" and "allocated"** by the leader of the village in the beginning of the history and this is how money should be allocated and "given" by the person in charge of governing his community to each member of the community who is in need of money. This is the beginning of the circulation of money.

Perhaps it is also quite probable that in some villages leaders did not treat their villagers equally, instead, they must have allocated money according to the size of family, industriousness, intelligence, assignment of labour, etc., thus varied the amount they distributed to each one of the villagers.

However, **one very important rule must have been common to all the villages that introduced money, which is to "give" and "allocate" money to each one of the villagers when they first introduced money and this was the only method to provide villagers with money in the beginning of the history of monetary economy.**

How about borrowing and lending?

The deeds of borrowing and lending come after the allocation of money.

We can easily guess that some one of the village would be in trouble for some kind of reason and he would need more money than he was given, and he would have to borrow money from someone.

But, again the first allocation of money at the very beginning took the form of "being given" by the leader of the village, but never borrowing or lending it from the provider of money.

Therefore, we can conclude here that money should be given and allocated to each one of the community (nation) by the leader of the community (nation).

According to what standard money should be allocated is another question.
What we have to focus at the moment is how the money was distributed among the villagers in the beginning of the history and it took the form of "giving".

Because I believe there lies a big pitfall in all the theses of economics or actual policies regarding the distribution and circulation of money, which is a crucial element in terms of stimulating and controlling economy, I should like to emphasize and repeat as follows;

Money should be "given" by the central government (the leader of the village is president or prime minister in modern nation) to each national of any nation when love and intellect grow and increase in the nation. It should not take the form of lending.

This is the very method how money should be distributed among the members of the village or community.

Let us keep studying how and when the leader of our village allocates money.

Money is to be introduced when love and knowledge grow in the village.

And this is the ultimate rule concerning when money is to be minted or printed additionally.

Money should be printed or minted when the population grows in the village or more accurately stating it, money should be printed when the villagers work diligently in order to grow, increase and improve their love for others and intellect among the villagers and such hard work might result in the marriage and births of new born babies, otherwise the demand for money will surpass the supply of money (that is the shortage of the circulating money) and the village inevitably has to go back to barter trade economy or the villagers have to rush and compete to grab the amount of money they need and that will bring in a chaotic situation in the village.

And let us confirm again exactly when additional quantity of money is to be printed?

It is, I suppose, when the village of five hundred introduced money, the leader of the village allocated money to each one of the villagers according to some standard (since mankind has always and steadily been growing towards a more enlightened state year by year throughout the whole history, the standard according to which money should be given is that the villager is working hard to grow and increase his and others' love for himself and others and his and others' intellect to cultivate the inner world of each one self and contribute to the enlightenment of the entire villagers through his skill one way or the other, and it is apparent that negligent villagers won't be given additional money) and he must have judged that more money should be printed additionally when a baby was born, the five hundred and first villager in the village, as a result of increased love and knowledge of the baby's parents. And then when five hundred and second villager was born in the village he must have ordered again the person in charge of printing (or minting) to print an additional quantity of money for the five hundred and second member to grow.

Babies can't spend money, so actually their parents must have been given the money as payment in modern term which they needed to raise their babies in accordance with their contribution towards the growth of the village through their work. And continually these parents must be supplied with or earn more money (in modern term) in order to raise their children, and the very growth of the children will definitely cause the further production of goods which these kids need and more money should be printed along with increase of the production of such goods.

However, the ultimate rule remains the same that when the villagers work hard to increase their love for others and intellect in the village (the ultimate driving force to increase population) and as a result population grows, more money should be printed. And who is the decision maker regarding when and how much money should be printed?

It should be the leader of the village, but never the person in charge of printing money.

If the person in charge of printing or minting money prints money at his own liberty without consent of the leader, there might be a possibility that he would print more money or would not print enough money than required and he would have degraded the village economy into a chaotic state.

So, the one who has to make a decision when and how much money should be printed is the leader of the village and never the person in charge of printing or minting money.

Interpreting it in our modern nation, printing of money should be controlled by the president or prime minister (or the central government) of a nation and the central bank is only to follow his decision, but the central bank should never be in charge of making a decision regarding how much more money should be additionally printed and neither in charge of controlling the quantity and amount of money that circulates in the nation.

In our modern world developed nations have established a totally different system of controlling the amount of money that is to circulate in the nation. Central bank has got a super prerogative to control the amount of money of the nation and central government is only asserting their opinions and requests on the monetary policy in vain, and because the central government is not given of any right to control money, central government tends to blame central bank's inability or mismanagement of the nation's economy when the economy is not running well.

However, as we have just examined, the amount and quantity of money that is to circulate in a nation should be solely controlled by the leader of a nation or the central government (in our modern world), and the central bank in charge of printing or minting money is only to follow the government's decision.

If we keep on allowing the central bank to control the quantity of the money to circulate and be accumulated in the nation, the world's economy will never get out of the chaotic state just as we are seeing until today.

Central bank at best may present their opinion or advice to the leader or the government of the nation concerning the management of the economy and the entire amount and quantity of money that is to circulate in the nation and how much money should be additionally printed.

(In this book I use the word "circulate" as meaning the total sum of the quantity of the money in a nation, that is both circulating in the market daily and saved in any household.)

Therefore, here we can assert that the leader of a nation and the central government must be solely in charge of controlling the amount and quantity of the money that is to circulate in the nation.

3) Money-lending

What we have to examine next is the deed of lending money and its disappearance which is very likely to happen in the very near foreseeable future.

I suppose there are many people believing that lending money is one of the means to increase wealth or the amount of money to circulate or flow in the country.

However, it is quite easy to tell that such an idea is entirely wrong when it comes to a nation. Such an idea is only applicable and does function in a private business and private life for a certain limited period of time in the course of human history.

The only means to increase the quantity of money is to print or mint money. (Being a non- native English speaker, I am almost ignoring the terminology, usage and minute differences between "printing" and "minting", "money", "coin" and "currency". Moreover these accurate definitions are not much required in this philosophical quest.)

Money is something which someone produces or manufactures by hand or machine, and money never reproduces money by itself. This is such a simple fact that anybody can accept.

Yet many people do fall into a false belief without consideration that lending money creates wealth somehow. Interest to be charged and paid upon the deed of borrowing money should be acquired somehow and from somewhere but never by printing money, and the entire quantity of money never increases on its own no matter how much money is exchanged for the purposes of lending or borrowing, if the central bank never prints additional money.

(Again I am using the word "wealth" as meaning accumulation of money. I know that "wealth" has something more than money, but let us just keep ignoring a minute difference for such a definition is not required in this philosophy.)

Then, what is the nature of the deed of lending money?

Let us go back to our village of one hundred (or five hundred or whatever number you may like).

We have examined that the village starts to invent and use money when the village can no longer manage its economy by barter trade because of the increase of population.

The money is to be distributed and "given" to each one of the villagers by the leader of the village but never by the person in charge of minting it.

And when does the leader of the village decide to print an additional quantity of money?

That is when a new born baby has joined the village because increase of population is the main motive and cause for the village to move towards monetary economy.

And we have agreed that this was the probable course of history that happened.

In a small village of five hundred, seven hundred, one thousand it is not hard to grasp exactly when and how many babies are born in the village.

However, we can imagine that it would become increasingly difficult to grasp the exact figure of the village as population increases (when the village grows into a bigger size so as to make the villagers unable to grasp its exact figure in a moment, it is no longer a village, but it is better to be called city, or the beginning of a nation, though there is no clear definition of how big a nation should be).

But if the leader of the village (or a nation) fails to supply the quantity of money that is required for the new born babies, the economy of the village would be affected badly. And yet the parents of the babies are definitely in need of money to raise their babies.

Perhaps in such a case the most probable situation we can imagine is that some one of the wealthy neighbourers would offer the parents to use his money temporarily until the leader of the village grasps the exact number of the new born babies and orders to print the additional amount of money.

Now we have found out how and when the deed of money-lending was generated in the course of human history.

What we have just examined is that money-lending and money-lender is generated when the leader of the village (or the nation) can't grasp the exact figure of the village, especially its increase and decrease of the population of the village, and the money-lender is acting as supplier of money on behalf of the leader of the village (and the person in charge of printing money) until the additionally required amount of money is printed and supplied by the leader.

Therefore, we can conclude that money-lender and the deed of money-lending were generated out of the time lag, time difference between the moment when the babies are born in the village and the time when the leader of the village correctly grasps the number of the new born babies (and including the recently dead villagers) and decides the amount of money to be printed additionally.

But if the technology was there to grasp the exact figure of the nation in a moment at anytime, we can assert that there is no time lag that tolerates any one to make money or profit out of lending money.

In other words, **it is lack of the technology to gather the statistical figure of population of the village in an instant, which generates, tolerates or allows money-lenders to come into being.**

Therefore, it is also just to conclude that when the technology in the field of statistics improves and the leaders of nations can grasp the statistical figures of their nations correctly at the speed of light if possible, it is quite reasonable that the very ground which caused the deed of money-lending and money-lenders will perish in a moment from this earthly world.

Actually we are facing such a situation in our modern world in which internet technology (information technology) has been dramatically improved.

And improvement of IT naturally fosters and leads the advancement of statistical technology as well, and it is also quite logical and natural that the improvement of IT and statistical technology will wipe out the environment in which money-lending and money-lenders can survive.

Nobody can stop this rapid advancement of IT and it is only a matter of time that IT will spread out to every village, every house, every corner of the world, which inevitably forces bankers to give up lending money and change the style of their business.

In Japan the upper limit of the interest rate which the law allows bankers and any money lenders to charge has recently sharply fallen from 29.5% down to 20%. The market of money lending has been shrinking in Japan and the number of money lenders has sharply fallen over the last decade.

Therefore, internet technology will indeed wipe out all money-lenders and the central banks' role to lend out money to financial markets and control interest rate to defend their currencies, and all the private banks of the world will transform from money-lenders to pure money-investors in the very near future.

Investment alone will survive as the only means for the bankers to supply money, and this is an inevitable course of human history when we consider the nature of money and that of the deed of money-lending.

However, some might ask a question;

"What if all the private banks never give up lending money and taking interest, even after the central bank ceases to take interest and becomes investment bank?"

We must recall that the very nature of money-lender is the representative of the central bank when the central bank (central government) didn't have the technology to gather the information of the population growth in an instant at the speed of light. They were allowed to exist and take interest only as representative of the central bank at best. Once the central bank has got the sufficient technology and means to gather the exact figure of the population growth almost simultaneously along with fluctuation of population, money-lender will have no other choice but have to stop lending out money and become investment bank or investor, otherwise they will be regarded as stealing money from the citizens and will be punished by the society or by the law that will be to be enacted. The central bank will supply enough money for the new born babies or new arriving immigrants timely using the advanced information technology, so money-lender or private bank can only act as representative of the central bank to supply money on behalf of the central bank to the new citizens (new born babies or immigrants).

We can reasonably imagine that the central bank of any developed nation with, for instance, a population of 127million like Japan can never allocate the amount of money required by each new individual citizen, thus we would definitely need private banks to come in to play the role of representative of the central bank.

However, once the central bank declares that it has printed and provided enough money for all the new citizens to thrive in the country, how can private bank, the very representative of the central bank, refrain from supplying the money or take interest upon providing the central bank's money as the representative of the central bank? Private banks or usuries will be considered as merely branch offices of the central bank in such an environment where the advanced information technology has inevitably got rid of the very ground that money-lender can survive. Thus if private banks and money-lenders take interest while they are acting as the representative of the central bank, the central bank will never allow its branch offices to do so, and whole the nation considers them as thieves.

So, once the information technology has spread throughout a nation, all the private banks and money-lenders will transform themselves from interest-taking institutions into investment banks that will take risks and dividend out of the businesses in which they will invest as the representative of the central bank, or they have to give up existing as bankers.
Or we might face another question;
"What happens if the governments and central banks of nations never give up the monetary policy based on controlling interest, even after information technology and statistics technology have reached the level where they can grasp their nations' true statistical figure (population growth and decrease) in an instant?"
The question is quite understandable because disappearance of the very ground which allowed the deed of money lending to thrive may not automatically and immediately lead to the governments' decision to end their current monetary policy. They will need certain duration of time to accept the dire situation they will be facing that their traditional method and understanding of economy of this world is no longer available.

Here is my answer to such a question that if governments of nations never give up the current, conventional financial policy, what we will face might be a revolutionary attack by the poor people upon the rich people and their riotous abandonment of labours and services to the rich people.

As the world population has been growing, the competition to get money for survival will be keener and keener, if the central governments never supply enough money by printing money and stop the habit of taking interest, all the nations' economy will face an ever growing demand for money and even be in danger of going back to the state of barter trade. And it will become very vividly and miserably apparent that nations will be divided into two parts; haves and not-haves of money.

And if central governments never print money but keep controlling money tight (it is happening slowly world-wide now), since the population of not-haves definitely overwhelms that of haves and once some leaders of not haves stand up to fight against haves, an all-out revolution will assault haves. But this situation has already been happening time to time in developing nations but the time for such a revolution is approaching even in developed countries.

One of the examples can be found in Japan where the drastic change of government took place in 2009. The true nature of the change is that the former ruling party had been representing only the rich people for many decades since after the war and the not-haves had been neglected in the politics and they stood up to change such a situation but Japan is facing an overall deflation and the population growth (demand for money) has already ceased, the central bank can't print more money, so, there has not occurred any situation that people rush and compete to usurp money.

But if the population were growing, Japan must have faced a serious competition to get money which could be fiercer than what is happening now, because the central bank never supplies money to the economy by printing it. (The Prime Minister Abe has launched his economy policy "Abenomics" to boost Japan's economy by pumping more money through the central bank. However, we must remember that the total population of Japan has been decreasing over the decades, so the policy to boost economy without increasing population will end up in a failure only with inflation of Japanese Yen creeping up and that will throw the Japanese lives into a miserable state.)

So, what Japan will need in the near future is a quiet revolution to stop controlling interest rate and abandon the monetary policy based on it and to start investment-based management of economy, as the nation has been improving its technology concerning statistics and this improvement of technology will inevitably urge the then central government and central bank to stop the current monetary policy for sure, otherwise even the quiet Japanese people will be angry against the then government in the future.

And business will transform accordingly. Imagine the village of one hundred, business in there is merely to reap what you sow, and in a village where the information of everybody runs through the village in an instant you don't have to produce more than required and nobody buys more than necessary, and you can't cheat anybody as everybody knows everybody.

Therefore the "business" in the modern sense, which tends to mean to get more than you need or are deserved to get or you tend to take more from and give less back to the party you are dealing with, will also perish under the environment where the information technology will have spread throughout the world as everybody knows who is doing what on the internet.

So, now we can clearly understand that modern "business" only spawned out of the age where information delivery is slow and imperfect.

And this conclusion proves that business is backed up by money-lenders. Therefore, once the deed of money lending perishes, so will modern business. And because business, always tending to make haste to gain more money (that is why it is called "busi-ness"), has been a big leading cause which has caused imbalance of the world economy (bubble economy and recession) and such a big cause of bubble and recession will end soon, the world economy will be very sound and moderate and free of recession and bubble but only grow steadily. In fact imperfect and slow delivery of information intertwined with growing population has also provided the environment for the various kinds of evils to spawn out on the earth as anybody who wishes to be negligent can easily escape from his obligation and responsibility of daily labour by hiding himself at the back of the multitude, but perfect and speedy delivery of information will wipe out such an environment in which evil or devil may creep in, as such an environment where everybody knows everybody functions better than the police.

Also it will become apparent that any profit of any business is merely the fruit of the growth of your love and intellect. Imagine again that in our village of one hundred the birth of the one hundred and first baby causes an additional production of goods he needs and this additional production brings in additional income and profit to the manufacturers of such goods. Thus it is even quite logical to say that the birth of your child is the source of your profit and the birth of your child is the very fruit of the increase of your love and intellect accomplished under the hearty cooperation with your dear partner. Therefore we are only reaping what we have sown. And this will be the transformed natures of the future business and profit to come after the deed of charging interest disappears.

Therefore, the monetary policy based on control of interest rate and issuance and dependence on national bond that accrues interest and the deed of money-lending in any form in private sector will be nullified accordingly, for interest that banks and money-lenders can take will perish soon.

4) Inflation

Inflation is a state of economy where demand surpasses supply and supply cannot fulfill demand on time.

Then, what is the origin and cause of demand?

That is the desire of human being to live in this earthly world.

This desire causes man to want many things required for survival.

When a man is matured, he gets married, and a husband and a wife need many things for their happiness and survival, and they want children.

And what is the cause of marriage?

Love.

And what is the cause of birth of children?

That is also love.

So, everybody is born out of love of his parents, and growth of population is also caused by increase of love and thus population growth also increases demand.

Therefore, we can conclude that love is the ultimate cause of demand on the earth.

We can reinterpret it as **"inflation is a state of economy where demand which is caused by increase of love surpasses supply"**.

And love in this case is the love for others.

But do we not love ourselves as well?

Therefore, we can accurately define that love has two kinds.

One is for oneself. The other one is for others.

And both kinds of love cause desire to live and they are the ultimate causes of demand.

However, when one lives alone and dies without spouse and offspring, his demand remains within the range of only his demand. He can be a Buddha with so much love for others, but in order to simplify the theory, let us ignore such kinds of exceptions. And we cannot allow such an exceptional case happens all over the world, had it happened so frequently, there will be decrease of demand and population, and humankind perishes quickly, as Buddha doesn't demand much!

Then, we can claim that love for others creates more demand than does the love for oneself alone.

Therefore, we must restate that love both for oneself and others create demand, but love for others creates more demand.

And when we imagine our small village of one hundred (or five hundred, or any number you may like), it is easy to imagine exactly when inflation is caused.

That is when love for others is growing in the village and new born babies are increasing and parents are in a happy state to produce any kinds of goods to fulfill their babies' daily growing demand.

This is the very moment when demand surpasses supply and the moment when inflation is caused by the growth of population in the village.

So, we can justly conclude that inflation is the state that love for others (cause of demand) is growing faster than the increase of supply in a village (or in a nation).

5) Deflation

Deflation is a phenomenon in which price of goods goes down because of over supply or of lack of demand.

Again we are going to delve this phenomenon philosophically.

Price of goods goes down, it appears at the first glance, because of the invisible pressure which comes from lack of demand.

So, manufacturer has to survive by cutting the price of goods somehow. This happens particularly under recession and this is an easy case to imagine.

However, manufacturer tries to reduce the price of goods even under a boom.

Let us take an example of Walkman.

Walkman was first introduced by a Japanese company, when and which company I am not sure, maybe SONY.

The first model was to use cassette tape.

Once Walkman was introduced by the pioneer company, its competitors followed immediately and the price competition was brought in as usual.

So, the price went down as a natural event of economy.

All this happened during the 1980's when Japan was enjoying its happy boom.

Therefore, we can claim that price cut or whatever you call it does happen even under a boom.

Let us continue the Walkman story.

The second type of Walkman was introduced by some company, maybe SONY again.

In Japan the second model (using CD replacing cassette tape) expelled the first type of Walkman very quickly.

Moreover, the price of cassette tape Walkman dropped sharply when the second type was introduced and even the price of the second type started to drop once it faced a keen competition with competitors.

This phenomenon also happened during the continuing boom in Japan.

What is interesting is that throughout these events all the manufacturers tried to expel the first type of Walkman by themselves by inventing the second better model of Walkman out of their own efforts and by their hands.

And this competition of invention of new model is still continuing in Japan and we have now the third or fourth type of model which is iPod type and even with better applications.

The price of iPod is now as cheap as the second old type Walkman or even the oldest models have already been expelled out of the market by the keen competition among the manufacturers by themselves and you can only find them perhaps in the shops selling classical goods!

And if you take a closer look in the research laboratories of manufacturers, what has been happening in all the manufacturers is continuous research, trials and errors of inventing new models everyday and intellectual competitions (over electronic technology) are taking place among professionals in the same division of the same company or even within the brains and minds of each ones of the same professionals.

And all this intellectual competition causes invention of new models of Walkman and this causes price-down of the old models and even new models as well regardless under boom or recession.

Therefore, what we can justly conclude out of this case study is that the very cause of deflation (price-down) is intellectual competition among colleagues or rivals or which takes place even within the brain of each individual engineer.

Therefore, it is a completely false belief that deflation is the cause of recession or you think you can find some country that is in a deflationary spiral or in a state of deflation.

This phenomenon happens where intellectual competition is keen and it does always happen wherever one single human being is there and it has been deflating all over the world since the beginning of the history as man always wants to contrive some kind of device, tool or machine, and continuously wants to upgrade what others have invented or what he had invented previously by himself or even what he has just invented a minute ago and he never ceases to do so till he departs this earthly world.

Therefore, we should state that deflation is another name of intellectual competition and improvement which is an intrinsic nature of any human being as far as he is a human.

So, deflationary economy as a general economic trend or tendency (thus widely believed to exist and haunt around the world, particularly in Japan) is only an illusion and it never exists. This phenomenon appears when intellectual competition takes place in the invention, improvement and manufacture of any goods, service, system or machine but it never happens nationwide out of any single one cause that cover the whole nation's economy.

Deflation is something that has been there all over the world even under booms, and in the case of Japan deflation appears all over the country because intellectual competition has never stopped everywhere in the country and even been getting stronger day by day and simultaneously demand has fallen short but "not because it is a deflationary economy nationwide".

And what is the cause of demand?

That is love for others.

Therefore, we can simply conclude that in Japan, the economy of which is categorized as deflationary one, love for others had decreased or ceased to grow as much as before, instead, intellectual competition in every goods of every field and industry, which was hidden beneath the bubble economy but actually had been there since the beginning of the history and is and will be active in the country, has come up to the surface of the country because the lack of demand or in our term love for others, which is the cause of inflation, has become apparent in the country.

This is the true state of the so called deflationary economy of Japan.

And lack or loss of love for others equals to loss of growing demand and it accelerates deflation (price-down to survive harsh competitions which is getting keener everyday) and recession as well.

But internet and information technology is improving day by day and it naturally nullifies the management of economy based on control of interest rate and dependence on issuance of national bond that accrues interest as we have seen, but the government of Japan has not acquired the future style of management of economy (to be solely run by investment) in its hand yet, thus accelerating the saddening sate of the nation day by day without any solutions.

Coming back to the point, deflation can be seen everywhere where human is there and it never ceases to be there because desire to improve his intellect is an intrinsic nature of human being.

And if we still take a closer look at the cause of deflation, as I have just stated above, intellectual improvement or competition is caused by the "desire" to improve intellect of oneself.

Therefore, we should state that deflation is caused by the everlastingly continuing and increasing desire to improve one's intellect.

Inflation is desire to love someone or to live with someone or enlarge oneself in others. Deflation is desire to improve one's intellect and the life of the mankind on this earthly world, and it happens in each individual's brain.

If you only love yourself, your intellect naturally follows your desire to live happily within a small world of your limited self.

But if you want to love others, your intellect again naturally follows your will and your intellect is used for others and for the common good.

Thus, love and intellect are always intertwined and growing hand in hand, and economy is only a phenomenon reflecting balance of desires of human beings.

This is the true natures of economy, and inflation and deflation.

Thus, deflation has been fostering civilization throughout the history to improve towards de-materialisation or spiritualisation.

We, human beings, have discovered various countless things and truths in various fields and explored this material earthly world since the beginning of the history and all the discoveries, inventions and explorations are owed to the brilliant work of human intellects.

Now that we have already explored the material world, we are going into the age of space and spiritual world.

And all this upgrading of civilization has always been caused by deflation which is the desire to intellectually improve human life on this earth, and it naturally leads us to the age of de-materialisation (the age of space and spirit).

In short deflation causes de-materialisation of this earthly material world or it should be defined that it is in itself the disguised phenomenon of de-materialisation of this world and planet or the ultimate driving force to cause spiritualisation of the life of the mankind.

In the age of space and spiritual exploration we need to grasp nature of economy from an angle different from the traditional one as I suppose conventional economics will not catch up entirely with the latest trend of the world, and I hope that this book will cast a new light.

PART II. Justice & Love

6) Justice and Love

I have learnt much from Plato's books and philosophical dialogues between Socrates and his deciphers depicted in his books.

The biggest philosophical theme which Plato searched throughout his life was "justice".

What is justice?

How justice is to be realized in this earthly world?

How does justice appear in one's soul?

These are the main questions Plato repeatedly asked in his dialogues.

In his masterpiece he attempted to find out what justice is through dialogues and study it in an imaginary nation, then proceeded to examine it in human soul, since human soul is very small but nation is enlarged convergence of human souls where you can find justice easily.

Thus, he started to build a nation in his "Republic".

In "Republic" Socrates (as Plato never appears himself in his dialogues and he made Socrates the main interlocutor) starts to ask;

"A city, I take it, comes into being because each of us is not self-sufficient but needs many things. Can you think any other beginning could found a city?"

"So we each take in different persons for different needs, and needing many things we gather many persons into one dwelling place as partners and helpers, and to this common settlement we give the name of city. Is that correct?"

So, it is division of labour, role or whatever you name it, which inevitably caused a nation or city to come into being in his words.

Then what does happen if you do something you do not know quite well, or somebody else does something he does not know well?

Nation will apparently fall into a state of mismanagement, disorder and even chaos if it goes to an extreme.

Therefore, each one of the citizens must concentrate in his own work, and this is the very basis of the founding ground of a nation.

And justice can be found in such a state that such a nation is governed harmoniously according to the very fundamental law which is division of labour when every one of the citizens gets the labour suitable to his nature.

Therefore, Socrates (Plato) says,

"What we did lay down and often repeated, if you remember, was that each one must practise that one thing, of all in the city, for which his nature was best fitted.

"Further, that to do one's business and not to meddle with many businesses is justice."

"It seems that really in a sense appears to be justice to do one's own business."

So, "mind your own business" is justice and not to interfere with others.

This is the definition of the Platonic justice. (The term of the justice we use in our modern world is a bit different form the definition of Platonic justice. And I would like to follow the Platonic meaning of justice in this book.)

Now then, how would you find out and define which work is best fitted for your own nature?

Can anyone carry on the work which he doesn't like?

Can anyone force himself to continue doing something he doesn't like to do?

Or is it not very easy to do something you quite don't like for many hours without taking a rest?

So, I can fairly claim that something best fits your own nature is something you like to do, something you can do no matter how hard it is or something for which you are willing and dare to take any risks to achieve it.

Therefore, the work which best fits your own nature is the work you most like to do, and since justice is, according to Plato, to practise one thing which is best fitted for you, justice is also to do one thing which you most like to do.

By the way, Emanuel Swedenborg, a prodigal genius gifted of a super spiritual ability to visit heaven and hell in the 18th century, said;

"It is very difficult to change your likings in heaven" (for there is no sense of time in the spiritual world and you spend eternal time in a moment).

You spend your time as much as you wish in doing what you like to do in heaven without caring about passing of time since there is no time in heaven..

So, you will continue spending your spiritual life in heaven in doing whatever you like to do.

Therefore, heaven is governed harmoniously according to each one's liking.

But this heavenly law is exactly in accordance with what we have just found out.

And if heaven allows us to carry on whatever each one of us likes to pursue without worrying about time, we can also conclude that heaven is full of justice as well.

And heaven is the place where it is full of love of God.

Those who do not believe in the existence of God and love of God can never go back to heaven and those who never love others can also never dwell in heaven.

So, heaven is universally full of love and heaven is the world of love.

Therefore, if you carry on doing whatever you like to do in accordance with your nature without being afraid of taking any risks, it is the very deed of your heavenly love.

Even on the earth each one of us becomes independent by his gifted talent and such talent brings income, love, marriage, family in the end.

So, talent or ability based on one's liking is the basis of love, or we can put it the other way round that **one's love blooms as one's ability or is disguised as one's ability. Therefore, performing one's ability is to perform his love. (And we must not forget that love and intellect always intertwine one another, so, blooming of love also takes blooming of intellect, too, but I am now only focusing on the aspect of love.)**

And because justice is to practice what you are best fitted for and that is what you most like to do, and because to do what you like to do is the blooming of your love (and intellect), we can fairly conclude that justice is in fact another name of love which is that every one of us does his own work which he likes to carry on no matter how hard it is.

Therefore, if we realize the world where each one of us does whatever he likes to do most, we can claim that we have achieved the heavenly world.

So, the very pursuance of what you like to do is both justice and love. And heaven is the world of love and justice where you concentrate on what you are best fitted for.

7) Investment

In our modern world all the governments of the earth are trying hard to tackle each one of the problems of their nations.

However, most of their efforts are not getting any results.

This is because they are thinking that they can solve the problems somehow by spending so much time, energy and budget.

Problem in general is an accumulation of inability, injustice and vice of human beings. (Natural calamity is also another source of problems but is rather a disaster not a problem.)

And injustice, inability and such are all caused by shortcomings, defects, weak points and all kinds of negative elements and aspects of each one of us.

Nobody can ever attain what is not originally talented for himself.

If I am required to overcome my inabilities or defects, for example a simple one such as playing baseball, I will never be able to do it in my life, for I am not a specialist in any sport nor have I a good sense of playing any sports even for fun.

In short it is simply because my soul is not apt for it, I am not made for it and my soul has no liking for it at all.

So, I will never be able to overcome such an inability or defect no matter how much time and money I spend for it.

It is almost impossible to make me do it and if someone (for example my parents) wants me to improve the skill which I lack originally, such an effort will be nullified.

Likewise any government's efforts to tackle accumulating problems will never be successful in solving and overcoming any of them, as far as problems are originally gatherings and accumulation of inabilities of each one of human beings which have been piled up throughout the history of mankind.

Then, how do we solve problems?

It is much faster and easier to develop nations by improving citizens' aptitudes and likings than by tackling a mountain of inabilities of them which definitely end up in wasting so much time, money and energy in vain as every nation has already experienced it over the past many decades and centuries.

In short, improving strong points will naturally wipe out negative aspects either in oneself or in a nation.

And even if he can perform his ability, yet his weak point or shortcomings remain with him.

If every one of any nation performs his gifted talent, all the nations will be governed well like heaven and everybody will be busy in performing his ability.

So, any nation can attain a state where its people can perform their gifted talents all the time, though their weaknesses, defects or inabilities still remain within their souls.

But their weak points will never be exhibited to the outer world for they are busy in doing their best, and others will come to help out his weaknesses.

And he is helping such others' weaknesses with his strong points.

And this is the very state where heavenly division of labour is attained on this earthly world.

So, every government should immediately take actions to cultivate, improve and develop ability, aptitude, liking of each one of the citizens.

And this is the very mission of politicians (top leaders) of nations to shift the governing rule from continuing in vain tackling the problems (mountains of inabilities) to improving everyone's ability and liking.

Each one of us is given a certain role both on this earth and in heaven.

To help every individual to regain his place best fit for him on this earth is a heavenly mission of politicians.

And to improve everyone's aptitude, ability, liking, talent is the very "justice" and "love" to be performed by politicians of all the nations.

Now then, what can be actual policy to be implemented by governments of all the nations to improve each individual's aptitude and ability?

That is best achieved and realised by "investment".

Direct investment by the central government to each individual to improve his aptitude, or company's hopeful technology, new project together with job training, mental education towards self-reliance is the very policy which any nation should take to stimulate its economy and upgrade the life standard of the people. (But realistically speaking, we definitely need private banks functioning as branch offices of the central bank as we have seen.)

And poverty shall be solved through direct investment by the central government into each individual combined with skill training.

And in fact not being given of any chance to improve one's aptitude and to perform his talent is the very misery for each one of us.

Therefore, giving only money to those in poverty without providing any chance to train and then perform their aptitude, ability or talent always fails.

8) Summary

Let us combine all the philosophical discoveries in this book.

As we have examined, management of economy by controlling interest rate and dependence on issuance of national bond that accrues interest will be soon nullified because information technology (statistics technology) is improving rapidly day by day and it will put an end to the deed of money-lending which was generated out of lack of statistics technology or slow transactions of statistic figures of nations.

(The deeds of taking and paying interest are merely transfer of money within a community and never create wealth by itself anyway. It is imperative to print or mint money if any government wishes to increase the wealth and the quantity of money that circulates and accumulates in the nation, for printing and minting money alone increase the quantity of money.)

Therefore, when the deed of money-lending has ceased, economy will be solely managed by investment which encourages and fosters each one of us to improve our talents, aptitudes, likings and abilities.

And liking is the very expression or bloom of love of oneself.
And improving liking (expression and bloom of love) is resulted in increase of population (increase of demand) and intellect as well.

Therefore, investment in each one's liking, aptitude, ability will increase entire demand of a nation as a result, and the nation (the central government not the central bank) can print or mint more money (which is crystalisation of love and intellect) which is to circulate in the nation (any government can print some money to invest in each individual's skill training to improve his love and intellect, as far as he is learning diligently to improve his skill in order to contribute to the development of his country).

And it is easy to grasp that profit of any enterprise or business is merely the fruit of one's love and intellect which each one has added to the community which he belongs to. And it will be very visible that the very growth of one's children is such a fruit.
Imagine and go back to the village of one hundred, it is very easy to see that an additionally newly born baby and his growth apparently drive the production of any goods that the baby needs, and the additional sales and profits of the manufacturers of the goods in the village entirely owes to the growth of the baby. So, it is quite apparent that we are merely making profit out of the growth of the next generation, for if the village of one hundred never increases its population and remains the same, the village can't print additional money and profit doesn't exist.

So, the love and intellect you added to this world returns to you as money (crystalisation of love and intellect).

Furthermore, the country which is facing a high inflation can take policies to increase intellect and job & skill training of each one of its citizens, which fosters deflationary effect on the economy and such intellectual improvement and training will lead to curb the prices of goods in general by improving productivity of the offices and factories nationwide. After the prices of goods have been calmed down, surplus money accumulated in the nation can be invested in new industries and businesses.

On the other hand when a nation is suffering from serious deflation or lack of demand like Japan, which implies that love for others is decreasing in the country, the central government or leaders of the nation can take policies to nourish love among the families of the nation.

But we must study carefully what kind of remedies can be taken for the recovery from the deflation in such a country as Japan where the people are facing a heavy decrease of love. (But this is a very rare case when looking at all over the world. So, Japan is in a seriously dangerous situation.)
My main ideas of solutions for Japan's so-called deflationary economy are:
1. Accept a large number of immigrants from Asian countries and perform nationwide and higher stage of love for other peoples of the world. Acceptance of immigrants is a driving force to push to the government to print additional money required by the immigrants.
2. Mint money and invest directly into people's skill training nationwide rather than just giving subsidy away to those in need of money in exchange of votes.

This is how Platonic justice, that is to encourage and help everyone to improve his liking and aptitude which is the fruit of his love and intellect in short, is to be attained on this earthly world, and that is the very mission of politician in the coming new world.

PART III. Practise in Nepal

9) Nepal

I received a contact all of a sudden from Nepal at the end of August in 2008 when I had lessons of Japanese language to foreigners.

I posted a free advertisement of my lessons on the internet and a young guy called Mr. Rameswar Dhamala found my advertisement and contacted me by e-mail.

His main purpose of the contact was to ask me to help the development of Nepal somehow. He had been looking for someone who can help him to develop the country.

But I didn't have any idea of dealing with him anyway, so, I kept trying to refuse his offers during the first few months.

However, he was "obstinate" in asking me to help him any way possible to me.

So, we kept communicating through e-mails almost everyday and many ideas came up and disappeared by the end of 2008.

He came to Tokyo at the end of the year and we met for the first time in Tokyo on the January 1st and I introduced him to an owner of agriculture farm who offered acceptance of some agriculture trainees from Nepal to train them in his farm. He had accepted over some thousands of trainees from Asian countries over the past years.

Since then we started working together to take permission from the Nepali government to dispatch Nepali agriculture trainees to Japan but finally the owner of the agriculture farm got into trouble last year and the project has been suspended till now.

And the true project started after that suspension of the trainees programme.

And, this was only a beginning to establish our mutual trust and long term relationship.

One night I had a dream in the middle of September 2010 and heard a heavenly voice in the dream asking me or rather compelling me

"Why don't you go to Nepal?!"

So, I took the flight to Nepal once again (this was my second visit) on the

12th October 2010. (This kind of spiritual phenomenon happens to me often.)

10) The Project in Khalchet village, Dhading District, Nepal

After some research and discussion with Rameswar in Nepal I finally decided to invest a tiny sum of money in the village where Mr. Rameswar Dhamala is from and his family lives in. It is a very practice of my philosophy which I have explained in this short book.

The village is a beautiful farming village with lots of paddy fields in shelves in a mountainous area which is in the district just west next to Kathmandu.

It takes about three hours by express taxi from Kathmandu to the capital of the district and it still takes about two hours by trekking from there.

I told him that I would invest 40,000 Nepali Rupees (almost USD400-) to buy seeds of vegetable for the farmers to plant in the village.

The population of the village is about four hundred (about 70 households) and upon my offer to invest they summoned a whole village meeting to discuss how to utilize my money.

What they decided was to divide the whole farming areas of the village into four big areas and each area to be divided into ten to twelve small parts in which everybody of the village cultivates and enjoys the harvest.

There are two big families in the village and they agreed to provide a large area of their farming land for those who do not have their own farming land.

The villagers agreed to set up and officially register an agriculture co-operative body to foster this project, which is, according to the Ministry of Agriculture, still very few in Nepal, though anybody can register and start agriculture co-operative by law. (The body registered was named Manarupi Agriculture Co-operative, Ltd.)

Though the procedure took some time, the project started smoothly and they planted the seeds of potato, radish, cabbage, carrot, etc.

In the beginning I experienced an argument about how to start the project with my partner who was saying or the farmers were saying through him as they don't speak English and I don't speak their language. Their claims were that they would be able to get more harvest if they had modern plough machine, if they had greenhouse to raise vegetable, if they had a four ton truck, if they had chemically improved fertiliser and this kind of many if, if, if…

So, I told my partner,

"You must fight with what you have right now. Then others will come to help you.

For example, Japan is now a developed country but we were like Nepal about one hundred and forty years ago when we started a national revolutionary effort to catch up with the western civilization (in 1867).

So, just forget and give up dreaming of what you do not have at the moment.

You have to start fighting with what you are gifted of now.

You have rich rewarding nature, buffalos for milking and ploughing, irrigation systems all over the village though very simple. So, you can start planting vegetable right now and you must start it immediately without dreaming of so many ifs.

The more you become self-reliant without dreaming of what you do not have at the moment, the more helps from others will come."

Such an argument and persuasion continued for some time but I pushed them to start buying seeds and planting them. I believe this is a kind of mental education towards self-reliance.

Therefore, investment should come hand in hand with education (cause of deflation), and education towards self-reliance is not always found in the school textbooks.

It is the mental and spiritual education of how to be self-reliant for the Nepali farmers and this is one of the very essences and purposes of the project.

(On the other hand if I invest in Japan, I must provide Japanese with mental education and training to regain and improve love for others (cause of inflation) along with investment. The love for others required for Japanese people to perform in this modern age where we, the Japanese, have already gained material fulfillment, is to help the people of the world who are not given the chance to stand up with their own skills even if they are gifted of so much.)

Anyway, they planted so many potato, cabbage and other seeds in their land by the time I left Nepal on the 17th in November 2010 and they harvested an unexpectedly huge volume of vegetable (total of 21,340 kilogrammes mostly potato). The villagers of Khalchet were also surprised themselves at an enormous volume.

I visited once again this village in April 2011 and visited some houses of the farmers of the village with Rameswar and found in every house four hundred to eight hundred kilogrammes of potato stored in the second floor of their houses (second floor is usually the storage room of vegetable all over the village).

It was a big surprise to me that rich nature has rewarded so much to their toils!

Then, we faced another happy problem which is to sell out the vegetable!

I and Rameswar spent many days to think of how to deliver the vegetable and to where.

Finally Rameswar was inspired of an idea to sell the vegetable in Kathmandu market off season when the price of potato is higher throughout a year.

Khalchet village had a stock of about 15,000 kilogrammes of vegetable during my visit and it is impossible to sell out such a huge volume of vegetable in the nearest market which has the population of only 8,000 people who live in the capital of the district. So, when I came back to Tokyo, I transferred some amount of money to hire trucks to carry the potato out of the village down to Kathmandu storage house.

11) The latest progress of the Project

I invested again in the autumn of 2013 in the same village to assist some villagers who are eager to start their own "businesses". Their businesses are such as furniture factory with an engine, sewing machine and a simple factory house, or tailor factory with a tailoring machine at home.

I provided some ladies with some amount of money that enabled them to go through training to learn tailoring. I also gave an engine to be attached with a sewing machine for a furniture factory.

I visited them in the village in April 2014 and met some other "businessmen" who are eager to start their own goat farming.

After the big catastrophic earthquake in Nepal in April 2015 we have to reset the entire project but are unable to do so since houses were totally destroyed and reconstruction of houses is apparently beyond my capacity. So, currently I am waiting for the situation to improve.

12) Foreign Currency

I and Rameswar often have meaningful arguments and exchange opinions over the management of economy, politics, civilization in general, etc. And the last one we had was about foreign currency.

One of the worldwide beliefs that I suppose the developing countries might strongly hold is that they have to work hard to obtain more foreign hard currencies like US dollars, Euro and Japanese Yen and they tend to believe that acquiring foreign currencies can increase the economic power of the nation.

It is true that they can import more goods from overseas by the reserves of the acquired foreign currencies.

However, it is also true that any foreign currency never circulates and be used as national currency for daily use in any foreign country (except when a country accepts it as its national currency), and importation of foreign goods using the reserves of the foreign currencies does never increase the power of the nation.

Importing goods from overseas without industriousness to be improved among the nationals only makes the country dependent on foreign countries.

So, what developing nations have to do is to encourage the people's industriousness by printing money and to invest money directly into each one of their businesses, projects, enterprises or challenges with job training, mental education and management consultation, thus increase step by step the quantity of the money that circulates in the nation and strengthen the nation's currency by motivating the industriousness among their own nationals, for the power of any currency is entirely based upon the strength of love (often interpreted and disguised as the spirit of self-reliance and courage to stand up to fight the problems) and intellect of the people of the country.

We must not forget that currency is money and money is the crystalisaton of love and intellect of the people.

Therefore, exchange of currencies is exchange of love and intellect, and if a nation depends on the foreign currencies, it means such a nation is dependent on the love and intellect of the foreign countries. And investment from foreign countries has the same effect upon the mentality of the people of the country. So, do not call for more foreign investment.

Therefore, any governments of developing nations must go on their own ways to develop their countries by printing and pumping their own currency step by step (which equals to the increment of their own love and intellect) and thus the exchange rate against foreign currencies will naturally improve along with their daily efforts the very purpose of which is to depart from the dependence on foreign currencies and countries.

Foreign investment can definitely encourage the people of any developing country to work harder and improve their lives with their own efforts, and that is the very nature of the help from outside.

However, the help from outside can only come when the people of the country stand up with their own feet and start working hard. So, foreign investment only comes in accordance with the increase of industriousness of the people of the country. Help from others always comes in accordance with this universal law. Therefore simply waiting for foreign aid and investment does no good for any developing countries. Stand up and fight with what you have, then the help from outside will be heavenly arranged. This is the universal law.

Epilogue:

Each human being consists of love for others and love for oneself.

Intellect and knowledge improve along with increase of love (both for others and oneself). And intellect also has two types, one is to search and cultivate the inner world of oneself and the other one is to explore the outer world. Love for oneself and intellect to cultivate the inner world of oneself grow together and love for others and intellect to explore the world grow together. Thus love and intellect are intermingled and intertwined always.

It is only a matter of balance of both kinds of love and intellect that vary economies of each individual and each family.

And every nation consists of millions of humans who are living to love others and themselves and to know themselves and others and its economy fluctuates in accordance with variation and increase or decrease of its nationals' love and intellect.

So does the world.

Therefore, the world is simply balancing on love and intellect for others and oneself of billions of people.

Economy is merely a materialised phenomenon in which love and intellect disguise themselves as money (or wealth).

Human civilization started from scratch without any modern technology and it inevitably spawned money-lenders who never create wealth.

However, we have got the technology which will make such a deed totally nullified in the coming future, which is a natural result of advancement of technology and human history.

It seems that human progress has come back to a new beginning point where we will start enjoying a pure life where humans can perform the very best of their love and intellect without worrying so much about evils since evils naturally disappear where everybody knows everybody thanks to internet.

It is just like we have gone through one big circle of progress in a few thousand years and we have come back to a fresh starting point after so many bitter experiences and lessons and we have to start from a new scratch again from the ultimate and original query of how love and intellect bloom in every field of human activity in this world to attain a higher realm of understanding and enlightenment.

After almost thirty years of philosophical quest, **it has become quite clear to me that economy is only a reflection or materialisation of love and intellect.**

Therefore, management of economy of a nation entirely depends on improving love and intellect, which needs a balance.

Inflation is caused by the desire to love someone or to live with someone or enlarge oneself in others (this is for others).

Deflation is caused by the desire to improve one's intellect and the life of mankind on this earthly world, and it takes place in each individual's brain (this happens in oneself).

Therefore, balance of love and intellect is the balance of desires (love and intellect) in one's soul. And these desires generated money in the course of history.

So, in short management of balance of love and intellect (management of desires of one's soul) is the very management of economy of a single human being, which is applied to that of a family and even that of a nation and the world.

Investment by government to foster ability, aptness, liking of each one of nationals will be more important after the deed of money lending will be nullified along with the transformation of business in the coming future, for love blooms as and out of one's ability.

And love and intellect grow hand in hand. So, investment in one's ability equals to investment in one's love and intellect.

Therefore, stimulation of economy by investment is equal to encouraging or nourishing love and intellect of nationals, and it will be very important for economists to know how love develops itself in the soul of each individual, in a family and in a nation and to master

how love and intellect have been, are and will be intertwined hand in hand and improved in this earthly world throughout the entire history of mankind into the future.

Therefore, we can justly assert that economics is now transformed into philosophical analysis of love and intellect and we even need a help of spiritualism which is bourgeoning all over the world now and casting a new light upon the love and intellect of a higher realm. This fosters unification of every field of academy.

Or in other words this is the process of spiritualization of money which used to be grounded on a material, gold. Money departed from gold and became fiat money, and fiat money is based on trust in governments. And what governments of the world have to do now is to increase love and intellect among nationals as we have seen. This is the true meaning of trust in governments. Governments will be trusted when they successfully increase and improve the love and intellect of their people.

And this is the very beginning of a true new capitalism and the end of the current version will take place in 2023. A new competition to increase love and intellect will begin soon.

February 15, 2017

Nakayama, Kunitaka

Author :

Nakayama, Kunitaka
Tokyo Fuchu-shi Oshitate-machi 1-35-71-305, Japan
House phone: 0423-60-8031 (from overseas 81-423-60-8031)
Mobile phone: 090-5788-5682 (from overseas 81-90-5788-5682)
E-mail: kunitaka@utopia-limited.jp
URL: http://www.akademeia.ne.jp

ISBN978-1-365-77527-7

www.ingramcontent.com/pod-product-compliance
Lightning Source LLC
Chambersburg PA
CBHW021934170526
45157CB00005B/2313